I0160051

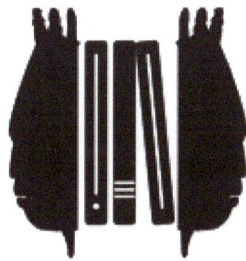

BLACK LEGACY PRESS™

WWW.BLACKLEGACYPRESS.ORG

ANANSI AND THE FIREFLY

AS RETOLD BY
UWA AFU

ANANSI AND THE FIREFLY

As Retold By
Uwa Afu

Copyright © 2023 by BLP PUBLISHING

All rights reserved. No part of this publication may be reproduced or transmitted in any form or by any means electronic or mechanical, including information storage and retrieval systems without permission in writing from the publisher, except for student research using the appropriate citations.

BLP PUBLISHING
Eastchester New York

For wholesale please visit:
www.BBWLogistics.com

Available wherever books are sold.

ISBN: 978-1-63652-121-3

One day Firefly came to Anansi the Spider's house and invited him to go egg-hunting. "If you would like to go with me, then come to my house late this evening." Anansi was very excited and immediately agreed to go.

2

When it was dark enough, they went out into the fields. Firefly would open his wings a little and his light would illuminate the eggs lying hidden in the grass.

Then Anansi would jump forward and yell, "Mine, I saw it first," and toss it in his sack.They continued like this for the rest of the evening. Anansi was so rude that he grabbed every single egg and Firefly didn't get a single one.

Soon Anansi's sack was so full he could barely pull it. Finally Firely said, "Goodbye, Anansi," and flew quickly back home. Anansi was left alone in the dark with no idea how to get home. Slowly he began to fumble his way back to his house.

He couldn't see a thing, but eventually he bumped into a house. He didn't know whose house it was, so he thought up a scheme.

"Godfather," he called out. A deep, gruff voice answered back, "Who is that outside of my house?"

Anansi called out, "It is I, your godson Anansi!" Just then Tiger stuck his huge hairy head out of the door and glared down on the little spider.

Tiger knew that he had no godsons, and he knew that Anansi had tricked him many times in the past. But Tiger was also clever, and said, "Come in, Godson," and shut the door behind Anansi.

Tiger had his wife put a big copper kettle of water on the fire so they could boil the eggs.

16

When they were ready, Tiger, his wife, and all of their children started to eat them hungrily. "Anansi, my godson, would you like some eggs?" Tiger asked. Anansi nervously shook his head. "No thank you, Godfather."

When the eggs were all gone, Tiger put a lobster in the kettle and then covered it in some leftover shells, so that it looked like there were more eggs inside. He then put the kettle Tricksters 12 on the floor and said, "You should stay for the night, Godson," and grinned so that all of his sharp, gleaming teeth were showing.

During the night, when everyone fell asleep, Anansi crept over to the kettle and reached inside. As soon as he did so, the lobster pinched him hard and he yelled out in surprise. "Godson," Tiger called out, "are you alright?" Anansi answered back, "I was bitten by a dog-flea. Please excuse me, Godfather!"

After a few minutes he tried again to grab an egg and received another pinch. "Godson, are you sure that you are alright?" Anansi responded, "Oh, Godfather, these dog-fleas are eating me alive."

24

Tiger sat up and shouted at the top of his voice, "Dog-fleas?! How dare you accuse us of having dog-fleas in this fine house, after we have fed you and given you a place to sleep!" Tiger jumped out of bed roaring and started to come after Anansi.

Anansi then flew out of bed and raced out the door, terrified for his life. Tiger came to the door and smiled to himself as he watched the poor little spider running away.

Anansi never went back to Tiger's house and every time he went to visit Firefly, his wife told Anansi that her husband was gone and to please come back next month.

'Anansi never did figure out where the field was where all of the eggs were hidden, and he had much time to think about how his greediness had left him with nothing.

www.ingramcontent.com/pod-product-compliance
Lightning Source LLC
Chambersburg PA
CBHW061058090426
42742CB00002B/85